Going on a
on a
TRIP.

what
FUN!

Revised and Updated Second Edition

Kid's Travel Fun Book

Draw. Make Stuff.
Play games. Have
fun for hours!

LORIS and MARLIN BREE

MARLOR PRESS
ST. PAUL, MINNESOTA

Kid's Travel Fun Book

Revised and Updated
Second Edition

by Loris and Marlin Bree

Illustrations by Marlin Bree
Cover design by Theresa Gedig

ISBN-13: 978-1-892147-13-4

Printed in the U.S.A.

MARLOR PRESS, INC.
4304 Brigadoon Drive
Saint Paul, MN 55126

CONTENTS

Look at all
the fun things
you can do
on your trip

GOING
ON A
TRIP?

GREAT!

Where are you going?

_____

HEY! Where is it located?

_____

Your adult can help you here

LUCKY ME! I'LL BE GOING BY
(Circle the right one)

BALLOON

PLANE

TRAIN

CAR

SHIP

OR
DOGSLED

Jest joking!

I'll be gone
this long

_____

days

These people will be coming
with me *(Lucky Them!)*

WHAT I WANT TO DO ON THIS TRIP

My list of things I
want to see or do

*(You can do a little research on your trip
on the Internet, in books, or in the library.)*

1/ _____

2/ _____

3/ _____

4/ _____

5/ _____

WHICH BUG IS DIFFERENT?

ANSWER: The third bug from the left doesn't have a headlight. If you see one on the way, you can play "slug bug." Lightly hit your companion on the shoulder, after you holler "slug bug." "Fun, huh?

DANDY ROAD SIGNS

Here are some fun signs. One of the signs below
is a real sign. Can you pick out the real one?

**DISAGREE
ZONE**

**NO RAIN
PERMITTED TODAY**

**DO NOT FEED
THE DINOSAUR**

**STOP RIGHT
NOW!**

**BEAM ME
UP, SCOTTY**

**CHECK YOUR MAP.
YOU MAY BE OFF THE
ROUTE**

The STOP SIGN is the real one. Look for its white letters on a red face.

WHAT I WANT TO TAKE ALONG TO HAVE FUN

1/ --

2/ --

3/ --

Suggestions: Take along a **pencil** or a **pen** to write in this book. Also take along a piece of string for string games and bring some sheets of paper to make folded things. If you've got a box of colored pencils you also can color in this book.

I GOT IT ALL FIGURED OUT. THE NEXT STOP IS FOR ICE CREAM! RIGHT?

BE YOUR OWN NAVIGATOR

Hey! Figure out all sorts of stuff about your trip with a map

If you know how to look, you can tell a lot from a map. Maps are just scaled down pictures of the real world. They've got lots of information for you to use on your trip. With a map you can find out all sorts of interesting stuff: Which way you're going, where you're going, and, how far you're going. Wow. You can learn a lot on a trip.

1. Which way do you go?
(Your direction)

Each map tells which way you're going. Look at the map on the next page:

☐ The map's top is **North**

☐ The bottom is **South**

☐ The left side is **West**

☐ The right side is **East**

Ask an adult for a map that'll be used on your trip. Carefully unfold it and hold it in front of you. Which **direction** are you going on your trip?

GOING MY WAY?

_____

(MY DIRECTION)

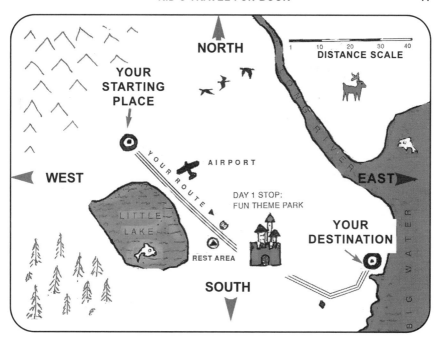

2. Where are you going?
(Towns, cities & places)

Have an adult help you find your **starting place** on the map. This is where you are starting from.

Then look for the place or places you are going. This is your **destination**.

Have someone mark your starting place and where you are going on the map. Draw a line between the two places. This is your **route.**

3. How far are you going?
(Distance)

Get a piece of **string** or a strip of paper. On your map, lay this between where you're **starting** from (your starting place) and where you're **going** (your destination).
If you are driving, follow the road you'll take.

Mark the string or paper. Lay it on the **distance scale** on your map.

Now you can **measure** the distance.

You can tell **how far** you'll go to get there. And you can tell how far you came.

OTHER THINGS THAT **MAPS** CAN TELL YOU

HERE ARE SOME OF THE THINGS YOU CAN SEE ON A MAP

DAY 1 STOP: HAPPY GO LUCKY THEME PARK

YES

YOUR ROUTE

HISTORICAL MARKER

Fun places. You can find fun places on your trip such as the Happy Go Lucky Theme Park and the Historical Marker.

LITTLE LAKE

Lakes and rivers. You can see big bodies of water on maps. These are colored **blue**. Can you find Long River, Big Water and Little Lake on the big map on the next page?

DON'T FORGET THE ICE CREAM STOPS

HIS VERY OWN MAP

HERE WE GO

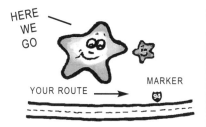

YOUR ROUTE →

MARKER
94

Interstate Freeways are shown on maps in red. **Markers** will show you which interstate you are on. Here you are on Interstate Highway 94, heading East.

Airports are shown by this airplane symbol. If you drive by an airport on your way, you may see airplanes landing and taking off.

5,000 to 25,000   25,000 to 50,000   50,000 & over

Cities & towns are represented by symbols. The shape tells how big some are.

0 10 20 30 40 50 60 70 80

A **distance scale** is important. It tells you how many miles or kilometers there are between places. By using it you can measure how far you've come and how far you have to go. *Interesting?*

HURRY UP!

Here's some handy information: a map will tell you when the next public **Rest Area** will come up. It's shown by a triangle inside a circle. You can do more than rest here.

I'D LIKE TO KNOW!

How soon will we get there?

If you measure the distance (using a piece of string or paper), you can figure out how far you'll go. Ask your adult about the distance you measured. Ask them to estimate **how soon** it will be to get to your destination.

HOW SOON WE WILL GET THERE

REALLY?

•••••••••••••••••••••
DAYS

•••••••••••••••••••••
HOURS

Maps tell you a story as you travel

There are different kinds of maps. The fold-out **paper map** is the one most travelers use. These show routes, distances, and things to see. They show states, cities, and areas.

Another kind of map can be found on the **Internet.** These driving maps show you routes and specific directions. You or your adult can do an internet search for "maps" and then follow directions to your destination. Hey, you can even call up a satellite view if you want to. Some vehicles have **GPS** maps, which show you not only where you are but show you the roads and some features. All together, you can find a lot of fascinating things in maps of all sorts.

How are you traveling? By car? Airplane?

How you travel makes a difference in the type of map you use. If you go by van or car, you can use an ordinary **road map** that is used by automobile drivers. Some vehicles also have satellite guided maps to help.

If you are going by airplane, train or bus, you may be going a long distance. Then you will need a bigger scale map. Some maps show the whole United States, Canada, or even the world. These are **large-scale maps.**

There's a map for nearly every travel purpose, including maps you can take on a wilderness hike or on a boat voyage. It's fun to learn more about maps and to find out what they can tell you.

ARE WE THERE YET?

Draw your own map
of where you're
going. You can do it.

Talk to your adults. Look at their map. Then draw
your **own map** on the next pages. *What* fun!

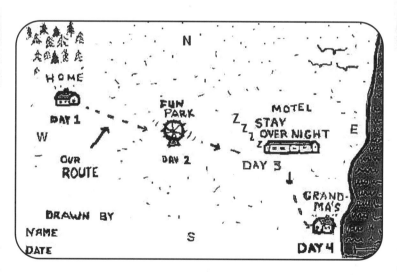

Here's an **example** of what a **kid's map** looks like.
The map starts at **Day 1**, *Home*, and, ends at **Day 4**,
Grandma's. See that there's a fun stop planned on
Day 2 at the *Fun Park*. Now draw your own map.
Your adults can help. Be sure to sign your name
and put on the date.

MY
VERY OWN
MAP

N

W

MY NAME — — — — — — — — — — — — — — —

S

Helpful hints: Draw where you will **start from**. Show where you'll be **going**. If you plan some stops along the way, draw those in, too. Mark any special **fun places** or attractions you may like to stop at. Hey, this is **your** map!

Draw your own map below. It's easy to do and fun. You can work with an adult on this. When you are on your trip, you can keep adding to your map. You can write in the distances you traveled, where you stopped, and where you stayed. It's a terrific record of your trip and your very own travel adventures.

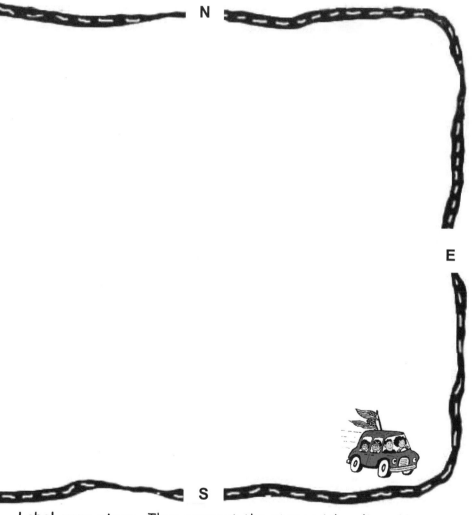

Label your stops. Then connect the stops with a line. Hey, now you've got your own route. This will tell you where you're going, where you are and how far you have to go. Ask an adult for information.

MY
FAVORITE
THINGS

Write down the things you really like to do while you travel. Then show this page to your adults.
(Adults: Take note!)

1. _____

2. _____

3. _____

4. _____

BE A TWO-MINUTE AUTHOR!

Each player gets a piece of paper and a pencil. When the Editor says **GO**, each player writes a story about his or her **favorite person**, without naming the person. This can be anyone the players are likely to know, such as a famous movie star, television personality, celebrity or author. When the Editor calls **STOP**, every one stops writing, no matter where they are. Then the fun begins. One person starts the game by reading the story, and the others in turn try to guess: 1/ What this person does and 2/ Who the person is. At the end, the **two-minute author** tells why he or she selected the person to write about. **Fun!**

ALL MINE!

YOUR
WRITE
&
DRAW
PAGES

You're the author. You're the artist.
Hey, this is your book. Have fun!

When you travel you'll see people, places and things that are not the same as they are at home. Travel is an adventure and full of special happenings. In these **Write & Draw Pages** you can capture some of what you see and do. You'll find these pages throughout the book.

On each **Write & Draw Page** you'll find a few ideas, such as writing about something special someone did for you today. Or what you saw that was especially interesting. Fun? Sure enough, and, when your trip is over, you'll have special memories because you helped create them in this book.

GREAT!

ME?

DRAW
SOMETHING
YOU SEE

When we travel, we see people, places and things
that are not the same as they are at home. Think
of something unusual you saw and draw it below.

A DRAW PAGE

WHAT I DREW _____

_____

_____

WRITE
ABOUT
YOU

HI!

Did you see a dinosaur? Probably not. But you can have fun writing about your own travel adventures. Your trip is special.

A WRITE PAGE

SOME HINTS: What happened? When did this happen? Where were you? What did you see? How did you feel? There are lots of fun things to say when you travel. It's an adventure, after all.

WOW

MAKE ZOOMY THINGS
WITH PAPER

FLYING FUN
WITH **PAPER**
AIRPLANES

A few simple folds and you can make your own paper airplane. Here's how to do it.

FRONT   BACK   UNFOLD THE PAPER

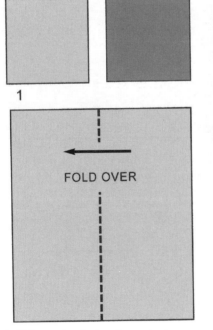

FOLD OVER

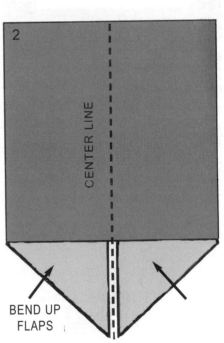

CENTER LINE

BEND UP FLAPS

1. Take a sheet of ordinary typing or other 8 1/2 by 11-inch paper and lay it down. Fold it in half the long way. It is now 4 1/4 x 11 inches. Right?

2. UNFOLD. Turn the paper over. Fold up the bottom corners to touch the centerline.

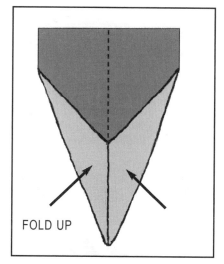

FOLD UP

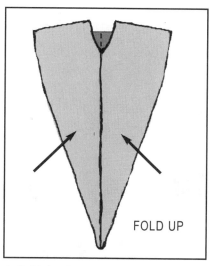

FOLD UP

3. Fold the flap over again. The fold should touch the center line. It's looking like an airplane, isn't it?

4. Fold the flaps up again. You have now formed the wings. It's almost ready.

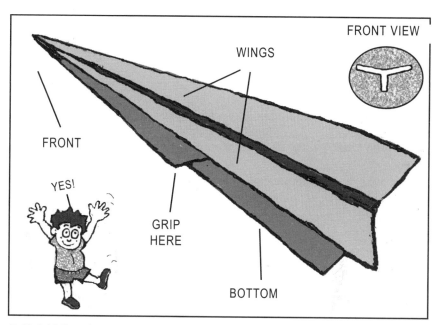

FRONT VIEW

WINGS

FRONT

YES!

GRIP HERE

BOTTOM

5. Unfold the wings once. They should stand straight out. You now have a paper airplane ready to fly. Grip it with your thumb and forefinger and give it a little toss. See how it rides the air? What fun.

NEXT PAGE: FUN GAMES WITH YOUR PLANE

THINGS TO DO WITH YOUR NEW PAPER AIRPLANE

GIVE YOUR PLANE A NAME. YOU CAN COLOR IT, TOO.

DRAW A PILOT. PASTE YOUR PILOT IN THE CENTER OF THE PLANE.

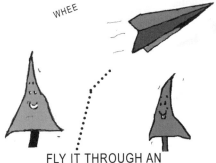

HOW FAR CAN YOU MAKE IT FLY? HAVE A CONTEST?

FLY IT THROUGH AN OBSTACLE COURSE?

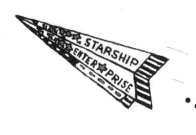

MOST HANG TIME – STAYS ALOFT THE LONGEST!

FUNNY? LET ME TELL YOU ABOUT **FUNNY**

WRITE
ABOUT
YOU

You've started your trip. Has anything FUNNY happened? Why was it funny?

A WRITE PAGE*

YOU'RE THE STAR

*HO.HO. ACTUALLY, THERE ARE NO WRONG PAGES IN THIS BOOK

AT LAST!

A REALLY
BIG PAGE
TO DRAW IN

(Well, OK, it's two
pages, but what does a
rabbit know?)

ABOUT MY PICTURE: _

_ _

TRAVEL IS AN ADVENTURE.

Every day is a new beginning. Look at
all the new people, places and things
you can meet and see. Travel can teach
you, if you let it. Remember that a
good traveler likes the journey as well
as getting there.

THIS MAKES
A RABBIT
HAPPY

I'M PUZZLED ALREADY

PUZZLING TOOTHPICKS

You'll need some toothpicks, sticks or pieces of paper that are long and narrow. Hey, let the games begin.

GAME 1: SERIOUS SQUARES

INTERESTING

HERE'S WHAT YOU DO: Lay down **12** toothpicks the way we did (above). You'll have **2** toothpicks at the top and bottom, **2** on each side and **4** in the middle. Got it?

YOUR CHALLENGE:

Remove **2**, but only 2, toothpicks but still leave **2** complete squares

DON'T LOOK NOW

...But the answers to the toothpick puzzles are on Page 30. See if you can work out the answers for yourself. Work with the toothpicks. Move them around. You can figure it out. Take your time.

GAME 2: NINE SQUARES

IS THAT RIGHT?

Count out **6** toothpicks and lay them side by side, like we did. You also get **5** more toothpicks to work with. You've now got a total of **11** toothpicks

YOUR CHALLENGE

Your challenge is to use **ALL YOUR TOOTHPICKS** to make **nine**. This is a tricky one.

GAME 3: BIG SERIOUS SQUARES

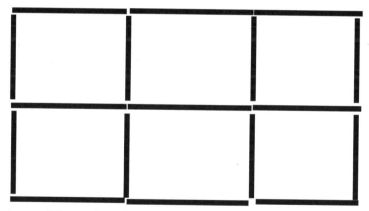

Count out **17** toothpicks and arrange them the way we did. That's with **3 rows** top to bottom, plus **4 rows** side to side. You've got **6 squares**.

WOW

YOUR CHALLENGE

Figure out a way to remove only **6 sticks** so that you end up with **only 2 squares**.

THAT'S HOW IT'S DONE?

AHA! THE ANSWERS TO PUZZLING TOOTHPICKS

(From pages 28 and 29)

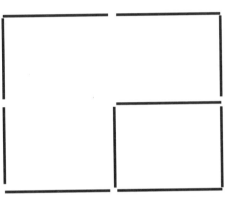

Game 1: Serious Squares: Take away **2 toothpicks** as shown. See? You remove the toothpick to the left of center and above the center. The result? You make **2 squares** out of **4.**

Game 2: Nine Squares: With **11** toothpicks, you've been asked to make **9.** Tricky? Take a look below. Add **1** between the **1st** and the **2nd** toothpicks. Do that again between the **4th** and the **5th** toothpicks. Go crazy laying in **3** more sideways to the right of the **6th** toothpick. The result? A really outstanding **NINE.**

NINE

IS THAT FAIR?

Game 3: Big serious squares: Your task is to take away **6 toothpicks** to make **2 squares.** You can do that by removing the **outer right** and **upper right** toothpicks as shown as well as the **4 toothpicks** in the **center** of the left hand box. The result? 2 squares!

WHOA!

FAST MOUTH

Game 1: Here's a game you can play without too much thinking. In fact, if you think too much before you play, you probably will lose.

To begin, one person says a **word**. The next person needs to say another word without a pause. The response should be a word that is connected with the first word. For example, the first player says *frog*. The next person can say *jump*. Or *green*. The next player says another word associated with the word.

Players say words quickly, one after the other, without repeating. The game continues until one player repeats a word, says a wrong word, or doesn't immediately think up a word and gets stuck with a *funny look* on his or her face. Ha!

NOT ME!

BAD MOUTH

Game 2: This game is played like **Fast Mouth** (above), except that instead of saying a word associated with another, you say just the **opposite**. For example, if someone says *stop*, the next player says *go*. One player says *yes*, the other *no*. What fun! (Especially if you're feeling a little contrary, anyway).

HOW DO
YOU WORK
THIS THING
ANYWAY?

HOW TO
WRITE MORE
ABOUT
YOU

Some helpful
hints and ideas

On the **Write Pages** and the **Draw Pages**, you have a wonderful way to tell about you, your trip and the people with you. Here are some ideas for you:

WHOO

Write about the Four W's:
Who, What, Where and *When*

Like this: *My Mom and I got in our car and headed down the road at 9:30 a.m. Wednesday (September 28) from Orlando, Florida. Our destination today is Disney World. (Wow!)*

LOTS

Check a map.
What can you learn?

Like this: Today we'll drive about 28 miles in our car. Since we'll be mostly on the freeway, we'll be there in about half an hour (the driver says.)

SAY
CHEESE

Write about something
interesting that happened

Like this: Just inside the park, Micky Mouse saw us and gave us a big hug. I didn't know he was so big (and so furry!). We took a picture. Nice.

Or write about something you saw that was different:

HI, GANG!

Like this: The Haunted House was spectacular, with ghosts and goblins. And then we saw this curious creature who said "hello."

YUM

You can write about what you ate (always fun)

Like this: At noon we sat at a picnic table and had hamburgers and root beer. The hamburgers were HUGE!

Or you can write about the weather

Like this: Today is full of sunshine and is very warm. It's pretty much like this all year long in Florida. It's hard to think that back home we have snow and ice.

You can write about any FUN THING you bought

Like this: Had to get a **Mouse Cap** with big ears. (I paid for it from my trip allowance. What a buy!)

IT'S **ME!**

GREAT!

You can tell how you feel

Like this: We all enjoyed today tremendously. It was great to be here.

For FUN you can grade your trip or vacation. You can write

Like this: On a scale of **one to ten**, today was a _____
(MY RATING

LOTS TO TELL ABOUT TODAY!

WRITE
ABOUT
YOU

Tell something that happened today that interested you

A WRITE PAGE

DRAW
SOMETHING
YOU SEE

EASY

Draw something you see
as you travel. Below,
write a few words
about what you saw

A DRAW PAGE

WHAT I SAW

TOTALLY
AWESOME

I'LL **GUESS** WITH YOU

FIVE
GOOD
GUESSES

When you travel,
it's fun to play
guessing games

1: How fast are we going?
(Don't look at the car speedometer)
My Guess_____ My Partner's Guess_____
The Answer _____ (Ask an adult)

2: How far will we go today?
My Guess_____ My Partner's Guess _____
The Answer _____
(Check with the driver or flight attendant)

S-O-O-N?

3: The time of our next stop?
My Guess_____ My Partner's Guess _____
The Answer _____

4: Closest to something
Pick an object a long distance in front of you. Close your
eyes. When you think you are alongside it, you yell NOW!
and open your eyes. You get one point for each right NOW.
Me _____ My Partner _____

5: When will we get there?

My Guess_____My Partner's Guess_____
The Answer_____
(After arriving at your destination)

BRACK

NOT A GOOD GUESSER

DON'T PET THE
STRIPED PUSSYCAT

DESIGN
YOUR OWN
SIGNS

You've looked at a
gazillion road signs.
Heh, Heh. Isn't it time
you designed your own?

1

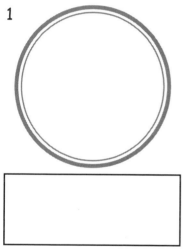

2

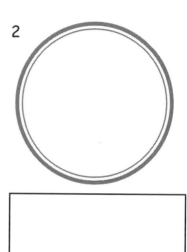

3

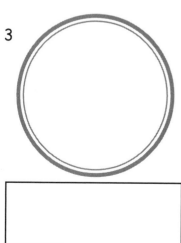

4

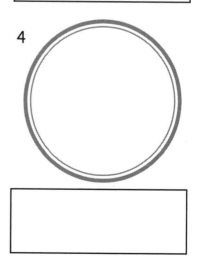

WRITE
SOMETHING
**WARM &
FUZZY**

Write about an animal
you saw while you
were on your trip.

A **WRITE** PAGE

DRAW SOMETHING
WARM & FUZZY

Draw a picture of an animal you saw while you were on your trip

WHAT I SAW

_____

_____

A DRAW PAGE

CATS RULE! YOU FOOL

MOON
ROCKET

Find the rocket that's on course and that will land on the moon. Hint: take a straight edge of some kind, such as a piece of paper. Align it with the rockets to see how good the scientists' aims are. You then can draw a line from the rocket to the moon.

FOLLOW THE LEADER

Game plan: Line up and **exactly** do whatever your group leader does. Here are some ideas: dance in your seat, bat bugs away, impersonate a frog's face (be sure to say *ribit*, like a frog). Or follow your leader to skip, hop or jump. Or try a high-kicking dance or play an air guitar. Or (under adult supervision in the swimming pool) make bubbles or dog-paddle.
You can take turns being the leader.

LICENSED
TO **GAME**

WHO, ME?

Your assignment, if you choose to undertake it, will be to see how many **license plates** you can see. Just mark an "X".

UNITED STATES

_____ ALABAMA	_____ NEBRASKA
_____ ALASKA	_____ NEVADA
_____ ARIZONA	_____ NEW HAMPSHIRE
_____ ARKANSAS	_____ NEW JERSEY
_____ CALIFORNIA	_____ NEW MEXICO
_____ COLORADO	_____ NEW YORK
_____ CONNECTICUT	_____ NORTH CAROLINA
_____ DELAWARE	_____ NORTH DAKOTA
_____ DISTRICTofCOLUMBIA	_____ OHIO
_____ FLORIDA	_____ OKLAHOMA
_____ GEORGIA	_____ OREGON
_____ HAWAII	_____ PENNSYLVANIA
_____ IDAHO	_____ RHODE ISLAND
_____ ILLINOIS	_____ SOUTH CAROLINA
_____ INDIANA	_____ SOUTH DAKOTA
_____ IOWA	_____ TENNESSEE
_____ KANSAS	_____ TEXAS
_____ KENTUCKY	_____ UTAH
_____ LOUISIANA	_____ VERMONT
_____ MAINE	_____ WASHINGTON
_____ MARYLAND	_____ WEST VIRGINIA
_____ MICHIGAN	_____ WISCONSIN
_____ MINNESOTA	_____ WYOMING
_____ MISSISSIPPI	
_____ MONTANA	

THAT MANY?

CANADA

_____ ALBERTA	_____ NOVA SCOTIA
_____ BRITISH COLUMBIA	_____ ONTARIO
_____ MANITOBA	_____ PRINCE EDWARD ISLAND
_____ NEW BRUNSWICK	_____ QUEBEC
_____ NEWFOUNDLAND	_____ SASKATCHEWAN
_____ NORTHWEST TERRITORIES	_____ YUKON TERRITORY

ME?

WRITE ABOUT SOMETHING THAT MADE YOU PROUD

Have you done something to make yourself proud? Did you help someone in your family or someone you know? Tell about what you did. (Always make sure your adult companion says it's OK before you help someone you don't know.)

A WRITE PAGE

DRAW SOMETHING THAT MADE YOU PROUD!

YES!

Draw a picture of what you did that made you proud.
Is someone smiling? Then write a few words below
the picture about what you drew.

WHAT I DREW _____

_____

A DRAW PAGE

10
PENNY PUZZLE

Get 10 pennies and put them into a **triangle shape** as shown below. The triangle has a flat base and a point at the top. If you don't have pennies, you can use pebbles, rocks, pieces of paper or other small objects.

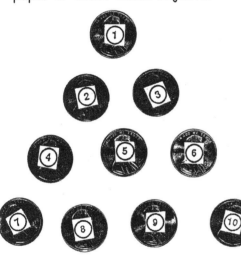

Your challenge: Change your triangle so that the base is at the top and the point is at the bottom. You want to make an **upside down** triangle, but you can only move **3** pennies. *Got it?* You can only move **3 pennies**. The answer is shown below. Don't peek until you try this puzzle yourself.

TURN OVER FOR ANSWER ⟶

Answer: Penny #7 is moved up to the left in the second row. Penny **10** is moved up to the right in the second row. Penny **1** (at the top) is moved down to form a new bottom row. Now you have an upside down triangle by moving only **3** pennies.

2 X 4

TOOTHPICK PUZZLE

YOU'RE DOING IT AGAIN

Take **5** toothpicks and arrange them as shown: **2** toothpicks to the left and **2** toothpicks to the right. In the center lay **1** more toothpick. You now have **2 triangles.**

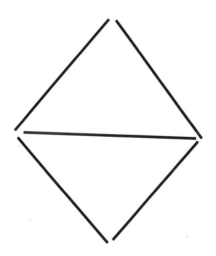

Your challenge: Take **2** more toothpicks and place them so that you make **4 triangles** out of the **2**. Can you do it?

Take your time! Play with the sticks. You can do it!

TURN OVER FOR ANSWER

ANSWER: Add **1** toothpick in the top triangle and **1** toothpick in the bottom triangle as shown. You now have solved the problem because you have created **4 triangles.** Way to go!

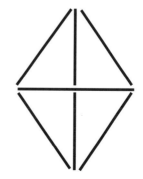

BARELY
BEARABLE.
HO! HO!

When we travel, our plans often need to be changed. Maybe a plane didn't leave when you thought it would or maybe it rained when you planned to picnic out doors. You can tell about a change you made. What happened because you made the change? Do you think you had more fun because of the change or would you have had more fun with your original plans. Bears want to know.

EXCELLENT

A WRITE PAGE

CAN YOU BEAR UP TO A
PICTURE?

FOR ME?

Draw a picture of some change you had on your trip.
Maybe the experience was even funny.
Bears like funny. *Ho. Ho.*

A few words about what I drew:

A DRAW PAGE

HUMM?

CAT'S CRADLE

Here's a basic string game passed down through the years. You'll see why it's fun

1. Get a long piece of string that is about twice as long as your arms. Tie a knot in it to make it into a loop.

KNOT

2. Put your loop around your hands as shown below. One loop is around your **left thumb**; the other around your **right**. Keep your loop under tension.

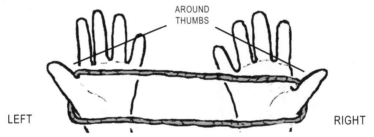

AROUND THUMBS

LEFT

RIGHT

3. Move your hand so that you put the string between your **little finger** and your **forth finger** on the **left hand**. Do the same for your **right** hand. Keep the string fairly tight.

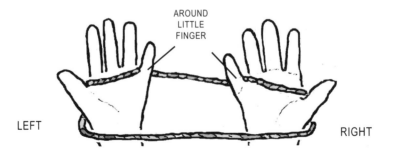

AROUND LITTLE FINGER

LEFT

RIGHT

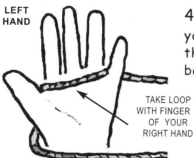

LEFT HAND

TAKE LOOP WITH FINGER OF YOUR RIGHT HAND

4. On your **left hand**, insert your **right** MIDDLE finger under the loop. Pull your RIGHT hand back tight.

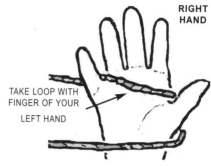

RIGHT HAND

TAKE LOOP WITH FINGER OF YOUR LEFT HAND

5. Insert your **left** middle finger under the right hand loop. *Pull back.*

SOMEBODY SAY CATS?

6. You now have a basic cat's cradle. See how it looks below. Neat, huh?

NOT ME!

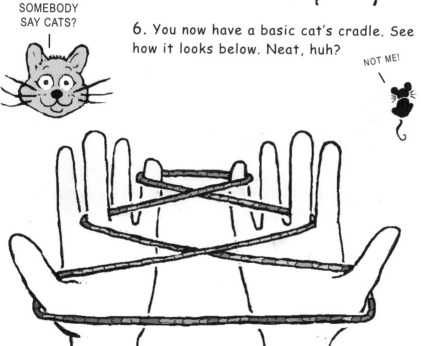

Practice your cat's cradle. You can go slow at first, then build up speed as you gain dexterity. See how fast you can go. Time yourself and see how much speed you can pick up after you practice. Show it to friends. Get another piece of string and challenge a friend to see who can complete their cat's cradle first. You can see why kids all over the world play string games.

ANYONE FOR A GAME?

PENCIL & PAPER
GAMES
FOR TWO
PLAYERS

START

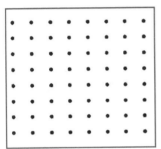

The Grid: **Here's** the grid you draw on a separate piece of paper. You draw eight dots up and eight dots across.

THE CAVE: Draw a grid of evenly spaced dots, eight up and eight down. Each player takes turns drawing between two adjacent dots. The object of the game is to draw lines which make a cave, but do not touch or cross any line to block a path. Each new line must join an existing line. The first person to block a path or be unable to move without blocking a passage is out.

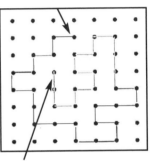

Gotcha! The end of the game comes when a player can't move without blocking the cave.

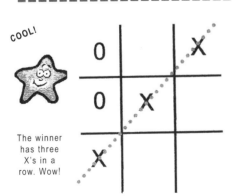

COOL!

The winner has three X's in a row. Wow!

TICK TAC TOE: Draw a 4-line grid like this. One player (O) puts an O in a box. the other player (X) puts an X in another. Take turns. Each player wants to get three symbols in a row, horizontally, diagonally, or vertically, while being alert to block your opponent from placing three symbols in a row. Try to guess your opponent's plans and block them.

FLYING BUGS

Hey, now! Volkswagen "beetles" are flying around, but they're not all alike. Find the two that match.

ANSWERS: Look closely, but Beetle #1 has no door handle 2/ no hub caps 3/ has rear bumper 4/ no antenna 6/ no headlight 7/ windows are white 8/ flat rear tire 9/ blank headlight 10/ only one wing 11/ black headlight 12/ no front bumper. Beetles **5 & 9** are alike!

FUN
WITH
CUSTOM
LICENSE
PLATES

Some people order custom license plates for their automobiles, vans or 4 x 4's. These plates show a name, a nickname, or tell something about the driver. Some are clever and funny. See how many you can find. Write them below.

DRAW IT

Games for 4 or more with **a pencil and paper**

1. Divide into **two teams** (4 people or more). Each team needs to have 5 or more slips of paper on which they write a **phrase, expression** or **title**. For example, you might choose **song titles, book titles** or **favorite sayings**. The expressions you choose must be familiar to all members of your teams.

2. Choose a member of your team to **draw pictures** (the artist). She will draw one of the slips of paper from the opposing team and try to draw clues that will get the other member (or members) of her team **to say** the expression on the sheet of paper. (But don't show the saying).

3. Everyone can talk except the artist. She can only **draw clues** or answers to team questions. She cannot use letters or numbers, so you must agree in advance to pictures that mean yes or no, for example. Perhaps a hand with one finger up is **yes** and two fingers is **no**. The goal is not to draw beautiful sketches but to make very quick and simple cartoon-like pictures. And have fun.

4. You can add extra rules: if the game moves too slowly you can allow no more than a 4 or 5 minutes to pass to guess the right expression.

 Ready, set? Let's go.

WHAT'S THIS?

Playing
DRAW IT
Use wit
and have fun
An example

Step 1:   Team one has chosen a book title (we won't tell you, the reader, just yet.) They give this to their artist who rapidly draws this picture:

Step 2: The team guesses it is a man. The artist signals OK, then proceeds to draw the following on the picture. Wow. It's changing. He's growing hairy. Somebody guesses, "hairy." OK.

Step 4: The artist draws the following round object. To make it easy, she adds a daisy. It's a flower pot. Somebody says, "pot." OK.

Step 5: The artist draws the next picture. Somebody says **goblet**. She adds flames coming out. *Got it?*

Step 6: Still a puzzle? The artist adds glasses. Like this. *Big hint!*

Who is it? Let's review: First of all, you've got this guy who's hairy (1 & 2). Make that Harry (6) with the trademark glasses. Then you've got a pot (4). And you've got fire coming out of a goblet. *Wow!* The answer is below. (It's a book.)

ANSWER: Harry Potter and the Goblet of Fire

ME?

DOG-GONE, WRITE!

It's time to write something about your travels. Did you have a special adventure that you want to remember? Now's the time and here's the place.

A WRITE PAGE

DOG-GONE!

DOG-GONE, DRAW!

Draw something you saw as you travel. Below your picture, write a few words about what you drew

A DRAW PAGE

WHAT I DREW _ _ _ _ _ _ _ _ _ _ _ _ _ _ _

_ _

YIPPEE

THE AMAZING
JUMPING FROG

Here's a fun little frog you can fold out of paper. You can make it jump.

1. Make a **square piece** of paper. You can simply tear off the top of a piece of typing paper.

MAKE IT SQUARE

TEAR OFF TOP

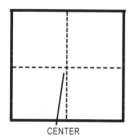

CENTER

2. Fold it in **half**, top to bottom. Then do the same thing side to side. Crease it sharply. Open it up. You now have a square of paper with 2 folds, giving you **4 squares**. Find the **center** (where the squares intersect.

3. Fold each of the square's 4 corners to the **center**. Run your fingers over the creases so that they are sharp. You now have a smaller **square**.

FOLD

FOLD to CENTER

FOLD DOWN

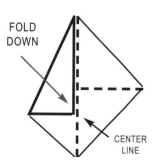

CENTER LINE

4. Turn your square so that a pointed **end is up**. Take the **left side** and fold it so that the edge comes to the **center line**. Do the **right side**. Crease them well.

5. Fold the **bottom** up **halfway.**

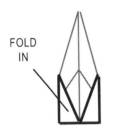

FOLD
IN

6.Fold the **left side** in to the center line. Do the same for the right side

FOLD UP
HALFWAY

7. Fold up the **bottom** halfway.

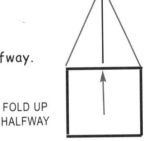

FOLD UP
HALFWAY

8. Fold the **bottom** square in half again.

FOLD UP
HALFWAY

JUST KEEP
FOLDING

FOLD
DOWN

9. Fold the **top downward.**
This forms part of the head.

10. Draw in the **eyes** and **head.**

HI!

ZOOM! ZOOM!

PRESS
HERE

11. Place your finger on the **frog's back,** near the bottom. **Press down** and slide your finger back. Watch your frog jump. Practice your jumps. See how far or how high you can make it jump. If you have a partner, see who can do the most with their frog. Highest? Farthest? Turn a somersault?

AMAZING
MAZE

**Help this family find
their way out of
the traffic jam**

You can go wherever there's an open space in the maze. You can't
move where a bar or a line blocks your passage. Start at the
beginning and try all the mazes until you get to the end.

BEGINNING

END

MADE
IT!

Don't peek. But for a solution, see the next page

I'M PLENTY AMAZED

AMAZE YOURSELF
WITH YOUR OWN
MAZE

On a sheet of paper you can create your own **maze**. A partner can also create a maze to challenge you. Just draw two sets of lines representing a place to follow. Be sure to include some dead ends. Mark one place **Start** and one place **end**. Test your maze and then give it to the other player.

HERE'S AN EXAMPLE

YOU CAN MAKE IT **MORE COMPLICATED**, TOO

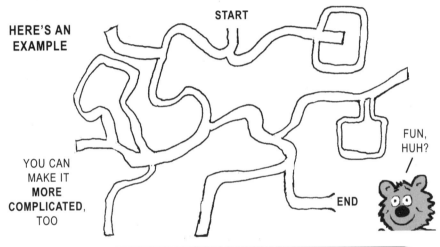

START

END

FUN, HUH?

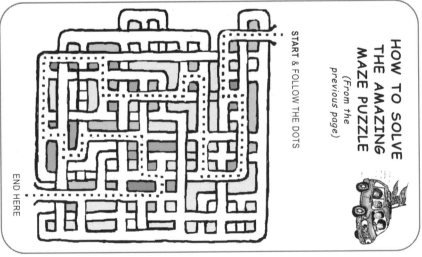

HOW TO SOLVE THE AMAZING MAZE PUZZLE

(From the previous page)

START & FOLLOW THE DOTS

END HERE

TWO GREAT CARD GAMES

FOR TWO OR MORE PLAYERS

CONCENTRATION

BACKGROUND: *You'll need a deck of cards, either regular playing cards or other cards that have matched pairs. Play this game when you're in your motel room or make a small deck of matched pairs for playing on the road.*

HOW TO PLAY: Shuffle the cards and then lay them **face down** in rows. One at a time, each player turns over two cards.

1. If they match, the player **keeps the pair**. A match would be any suit of the **same number**. Color doesn't count.

MATCHED CARDS
The number **2** is the same
(colors don't count)

I HAVE TO REMEMBER?

2. If they don't match, the cards are **turned back over**, but left in the same place. As more cards are turned over and then back again, this becomes an exercise in **memory**.

3. At the end of the game, the winner is the player who holds the **most pairs**.

HUHH?

WHO'S THE JOKESTER?

Another fun card game

HOW TO PLAY: Use a regular deck of playing cards with one **Joker** left in the deck. Or use other cards that have matched pairs and take out one card, leaving **one card** without a match.

1. Shuffle the cards and then deal them out to the players, one at a time. There will probably be some players with fewer cards.

2. Each player holds the cards so that the other players can't see them. To start, each player pulls **the pairs** from his/her deck and lays them **face down**. To make a pair, suit or color doesn't matter. Only lay down pairs. If you have three cards that match, keep one in your hand until you get another pair.

PAIR OF CARDS
THE NUMBERS MATCH

3. When all the pairs have been discarded, the player to the left of the dealer (Player 1) draws one card from the dealer's cards. Remember that you must not let anyone else see the cards. If Player 1 can make a pair, he/she discards the pair, laying them face down. Then Player 1 offers his/her cards to the player on the left (Player 2).

4. The game continues until all cards have been discarded as matched pairs until one player is left with the unmatched card: the **Jokester.** The Jokester, with the single, unmatched card, loses the game.

DUELING

WITH

DOTS

ON GUARD, ZORRO!

A fun game you can play with pencils and another friend. Just connect the dots

Zounds! You can duel with a friend with these **Dueling Dots.** Each person gets **one move** at a time between the dots. You can move up, down or across linking dots to complete a square. You can't move **diagonally.** If you see that your opponent is about to complete a square you can put your line in and claim the square when it's your turn. The dueling winner is the one who gets the **last line** in to form a square.

ROUND 1   ROUND 2

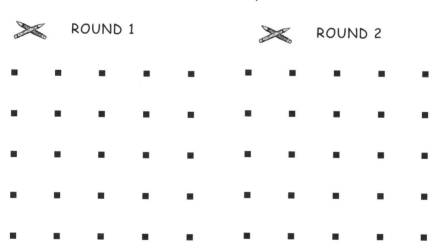

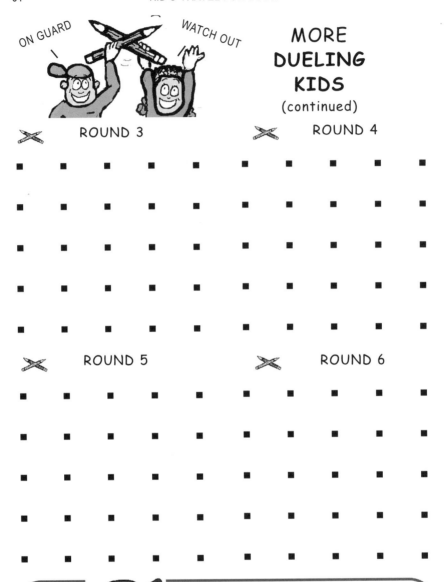

MORE
DUELING
KIDS
(continued)

ROUND 3   ROUND 4

ROUND 5   ROUND 6

THE COLOR GREEN

The main player picks something inside the car, train or plane (however you are traveling) which is a certain color, such as green. He or she then says, "Color me green," and in turn others try to guess what object he or she has chosen. If several rounds don't locate the item, then players can ask questions about its size or location. Winner gets to pick the next color and object.

MAKE THIS FUN
PAPER BALLOON

1. Make a paper **square**. Fold it in half. Open it. Then fold it in half the other way.

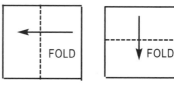

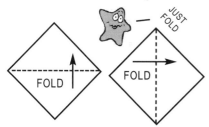

2. Open the paper up and turn it over. Put a **pointed side** up. Fold it from top to bottom. Open it up. Then fold it from side to side.

3. Unfold it. Using the folds as guides, fold it **inward** (1) so it becomes **star-shaped.** Flatten your star (2). You now have a triangular shaped tent. (3)

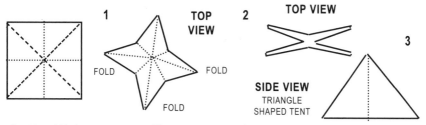

4. You'll have **two flaps** on each side. Fold the right side flap to the peak. Fold the left flap to the top. Turn the triangle over.

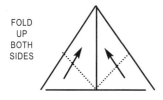

FOLD UP BOTH SIDES

5. Repeat the folds (right and left folds to the peak.)

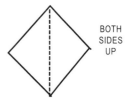

BOTH SIDES UP

6. You now have a **square** again. Put the peak at the top (the closed end). You again have **two flaps** on each side. Fold the **right** flap toward the center. Do the same for the left flap.

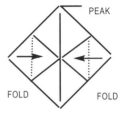

PEAK

FOLD   FOLD

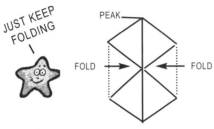

JUST KEEP FOLDING

PEAK

FOLD →   ← FOLD

7. Turn the triangle over. Put the peak at the top. Fold the **right flap** to the center. Then fold the **left flap** to the center.

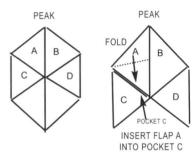

PEAK

A B
C D

PEAK

FOLD
A B
C D
POCKET C

INSERT FLAP A
INTO POCKET C

8. You'll see two loose flaps at the top: **A & B**. These fold into pockets **C & D**. See the detail. Turn your work over and repeat.

HUFF, PUFF

9. You now have finished the folding. Find the **hole** in the bottom. Blow hard. When you balloon inflates, help it round out with your fingers.

This is a fun balloon you made yourself. It's light-weight, so you can toss it in the air and catch it. Or bat it around. You can toss your balloon to a friend and enjoy a game of catch. You can play basketball with a motel room basket or a folded down paper sack.

ANYONE FOR BASKETBALL?

TOSS IT HERE!

A STRING TRICK

THE
VANISHING
KNOT

Amaze your friends! Astound your adults with this neat string trick. You'll tie a knot in a shoestring. Before their very eyes, the knot will disappear. Alakazam. Zow!

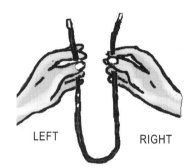

LEFT   RIGHT

1. Get a shoestring and hold **one end** up in each hand.

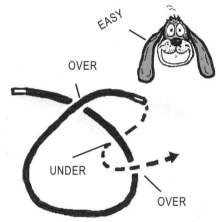

EASY

OVER

UNDER

OVER

2. Tie an **overhand knot** in the center. To tie the knot, just move your **left hand** in a loop around the string as shown.

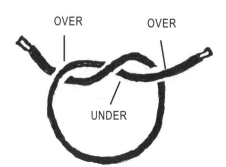

OVER   OVER

UNDER

3. You'll end up with a **loose knot** looking like this.

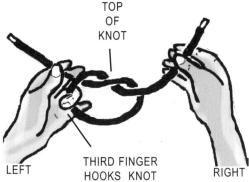

TOP OF KNOT

THIRD FINGER HOOKS KNOT

LEFT   RIGHT

4. Hold up the knot. Note that the **backs** of your hands are toward the audience and that your **left hand** is in a closed fist. Secretly slip your **third finger** into the loop.

5. This is what the audience sees as you hold your **left hand** above your **right hand**. Gently **pull** your right hand down. Zow! The knot *disappears in front of their eyes.*

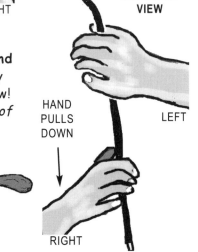

AUDIENCE VIEW

HAND PULLS DOWN

LEFT

RIGHT

LEFT

TRICKY

KNOT SLIPS

RIGHT

6. What actually happened is that, hidden from the audience's view, the third finger **lets the knot slip** along the shoestring as you pull. The audience sees a whole shoestring, without a knot in it, at the end. You can end the trick by tossing your left hand up as if throwing away the vanished knot. Then open your left hand to show that it's empty. *It's magic.*

HINTS: Practice this trick by yourself until you feel comfortable with it. The audience sees the knot you tie at the beginning, but be certain to hold your hands up high enough so that they don't see you slip your finger into the knot. By appearing to pass your hand over the knot, you make it vanish. Be certain to keep the loop loose so it will slip easily.

SAIL THIS
PAPER
BOAT

You can fold a piece of paper into a terrific little boat that floats and sails (if you supply the wind.) Great fun!

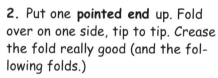

1. Make a square piece of paper. Do that by tearing off the top of a sheet of typing or other paper.

2. Put one **pointed end** up. Fold over on one side, tip to tip. Crease the fold really good (and the following folds.)

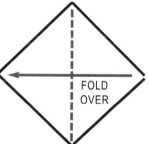

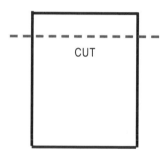

3. Unfold. The crease forms the **center line.**

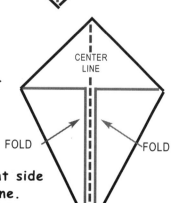

4. Fold the **right side** to the **center line.** Then the **left side.**

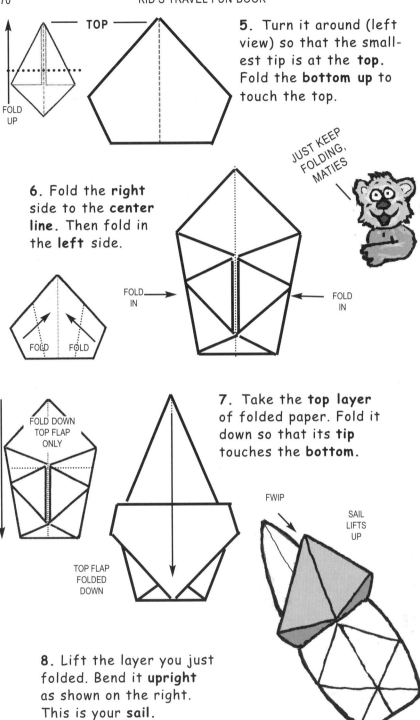

TOP

FOLD
UP

5. Turn it around (left view) so that the smallest tip is at the **top**. Fold the **bottom up** to touch the top.

JUST KEEP FOLDING, MATIES

6. Fold the **right** side to the **center line**. Then fold in the **left** side.

FOLD   FOLD

FOLD IN

FOLD IN

FOLD DOWN TOP FLAP ONLY

7. Take the **top layer** of folded paper. Fold it down so that its **tip** touches the **bottom**.

FWIP

SAIL LIFTS UP

TOP FLAP FOLDED DOWN

8. Lift the layer you just folded. Bend it **upright** as shown on the right. This is your **sail**.

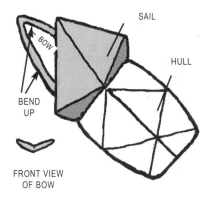

SAIL

HULL

BOW

BEND UP

FRONT VIEW OF BOW

9 . The bottom is your boat's **hull**. Bend the hull slightly to create a slightly sharpened bow (point). It should be a sort of V-shape at the tip.

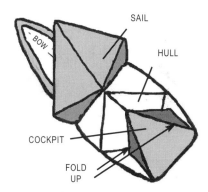

SAIL

BOW

HULL

COCKPIT

FOLD UP

10. Bend up the flaps as shown. This is your sailor's **cockpit**.

11. Give your little boat a **name** and **decorate** it. You can color the hull and the sail. Give your boat a little personality.

12. Put your boat in some **water**, such as a bathtub. Blow on the sail from behind. *Watch it go!*

GO!

Ideas: You can make a **fleet** of these little racers and share them for sailboat races. These paper boats will last in the water for a number of races before they get water-logged (depending on the paper). We used ordinary computer printer paper, but most any paper will do, including heavy wrapping paper. When your little boats get too wet to sail, you can let them **dry out** to sail later. And you can easily make some more. *Fun!*

AHOY!

DESIGN YOUR

OWN BOAT

Draw a boat that you'd like to have someday. Maybe the paper boats gave you a few ideas

MY PLANS _ _ _ _ _ _ _ _ _ _ _ _ _ _ _

_ _ _ _ _ _ _ _ _ _ _ _ _ _ _ _ _ _

_ _ _ _ _ _ _ _ _ _ _ _ _ _ _ _ _

NICE GOING MATEY!

GAMES
TO
PLAY

CLASS ACT

One person selects a **class or category** *(colors, movie stars, books, dogs, cats, birds, sports teams, etc.)* and each player takes turns **naming something** in that class or category. The last player with an answer is the winner.

You may want to keep a list of what's been named to keep from repeating names. The winner gets to pick the next class. Be sure to pick a **class** that everyone will know about.

CARPENTER WORDS

The object of this game is to build **as long a word** as you can. The first player chooses a **vowel** (a, e, i, o, u). The second player chooses a **consonant** (any letter that isn't a vowel) that will spell a word. Letters can be used more than once and can be rearranged. See how many letters can be added and still be able to form a word from them.

For example, Player One chooses an **A**. Player Two chooses **M**, so the word formed is *AM*. The letters are added on anywhere to form new word, such as: am, arm, harm, charm, charms. Got the idea?

FUR ME?

MAKE A

FRIENDSHIP
RING

Have a special friend? Here's how you can make a special token of your friendship with a Friendship Ring

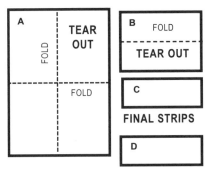

1. Start with a piece of 8 1/2 x 11-inch paper (A), then **fold it** in half, from **top to bottom**. Then fold it again in half **side to side**. You now have 4 quarters. Tear out (B) **one quarter**. Then fold that quarter from side to side so that you have (C & D) **two long, narrow strips** each about 2 inches by 5 1/2 inches. You have created the **band (C)** and the **crown (D)**.

2. Fold strip **C** in half the **long way** as shown. **Unfold.** You have a **centerline** down the long strip. Fold **each edge** in to the centerline. This will create a band about 1 inch wide.

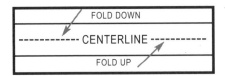

3. Fold the long strip in **half again** to make a long thin strip about **1/2 inch** wide. You have finished with **(C)the band.**

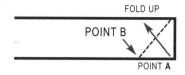

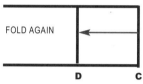

4. The crown(D). Use your second strip. On the right side, fold up one corner **Point A** to the top. Then unfold it. The bottom point becomes **Point B**.

5. Fold over **Point A** to **Point C**, making a **square**. (If you fold over at the bottom of the previous fold, Point B, you'll also have a square.

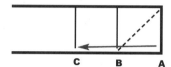

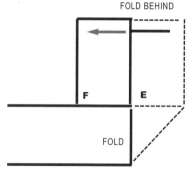

6. Fold that square over again, from **Point C** to **Point D**.

7. UNFold. Take the long strip and give it a **twist** so that it **folds under** to Point E. You now have an **L shape.**

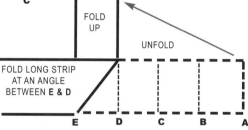

8. Fold the L shape again to your **left** from Point E to Point F. Note that the fold goes **behind** the band.

9. Fold the upper strip down as shown.

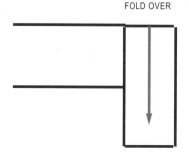

10. Fold up once.

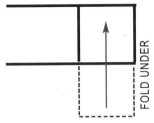

And **fold down** the end tab.

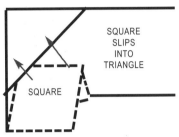

11. Slip the **square**, folded down at the end, into the **triangle** at the back of the long strip. You have created your own crown. Note you have a collar formed in front.

12. On the left side, fold the tips down to make an arrow shape.

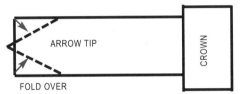

13. Bend the band in a **circle** and insert the **arrow tip** into the **crown** as shown. Gently squeezing at the top and bottom will help open the collar.

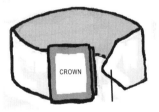

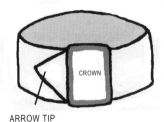

You now have a handsome **Friendship Ring**. Adjust the length to fit. Give it to your friend.

BIGGER OR SMALLER? If your ring is too big or too small, you can easily adjust it. Unfold your ring. Then add or take out another "square." (Step 6). Then refold it the same as before (Steps 7 through 13.)

DECORATE YOUR RING

You can decorate your Friendship Ring in a number of ways. Use your imagination.

LOVE IT

ON THE CROWN

FRIEND'S INITIALS

PICTURE OF FRIEND

TWO HEARTS

SPECIAL DATE

STARS

ON THE BAND

FANCY DECORATIONS

COMMEMORATIVE

A PLEDGE OR SAYING

ON THE INSIDE

YOUR NAME AND WHO
YOU'RE GIVING THE RING TO

A SPECIAL REMEMBRANCE
OR MEMORY

FUN
GAMES
TO
PLAY

LIVE! YOU'RE ON TV!

Take turns being a **television news person** on a live satellite telecast. To do this, the gamemaster identifies the **news subject** and says, *"You're on,"* and points to a player. That player then gives a **live** news-type telecast to viewers.

Your news subjects can be most anything, including: looking out the window at a cow, a dog sleeping beside the road, a horse in the field, or a car ahead. Anything fun like that.

The announcer needs to **deepen** his or her voice to sound official and talk importantly without hesitation (no *uhs* or *umns* allowed). An umn or an ah will put a player **out** as will a delay between words of more than a few seconds. A time limit is 20 seconds.

Ready? Set? Well..**you're on!**

I'M SO READY
FOR PRIME
TIME

I SPY

The person who is **IT** says: "I spy with my eye something beginning with _____. The other players ask questions until someone guesses the object.

For example, IT may say, "*I spy with my eye something beginning with C.*" The other players ask questions: "*Is it big? Does it give milk?*" The answer is Cow.

To make the game more difficult, you can include categories like animal, vegetable or mineral. The players can agree to limit the number of questions or the time before they must give up.

QUACK UP

Silly phrases are in! **Pick a phrase** and the next player has to answer **only** with the **chosen phrase**. Make up your own phrases in advance.

Here are some examples: *Beam me up, Mr. Spock. Lots of Luck. Quack, quack,* or *Look out behind you, Harry!*

To play the game, for example, someone says: "*Want to take a break?*" and the player has to respond only with the **chosen phrase,** such as "*Lots of luck.*" Take turns thinking up phrases and being the gamemaster.

20 QUESTIONS

Players may ask **twenty questions** to guess an answer. The answer may be a person, thing, place, title, etc. It must be something that all the players will know about. For example, an adult movie star or adult book titles may not be an appropriate choice when a young child is playing. To win the game, the players must guess the correct answer before they have used their twenty questions.

YES
OR
NO?

A *variation* on the games of **Twenty Questions** or **I Spy** is to limit the questions so that the player who is IT can only ask questions that can be answered by Yes or **No**. It takes extra thought to think of questions that will give you information when you play these games. (For example, was this movie about an animal?)

HI

TINY
PEOPLE
ON YOUR
FINGERS

WOOF

They move. They talk (with a little help.) And they're ALL on your fingers.

1. Tear out a piece of paper about **three inches** square.

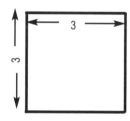

3

3

2. Fold up about a **half inch** of the bottom. This forms a **cuff**.

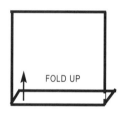

FOLD UP

3. Decorate your little person.

4. Bend your paper into a cylinder shape. Insert one side into the other. The cuff will hold it together. Fit it to your finger.

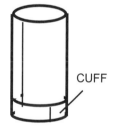

CUFF

5. You can now put on your own **movie, TV show** or **Broadway play.** Do one fig-ure or many. Best of all, you do the singing and the talking. You're the director. And the star. *Wow.*

HEY! MY TURN

COWS ARE GOOD

DRAW
SOMETHING
YOU SEE

MOO

Draw something you see as you travel. Below your picture, write a few words about what you drew.

A DRAW PAGE

EXCELLENT

.WHAT I DREW: _____

_____

_____

WRITE
ABOUT
YOU

Tell something that happened today that interested **you**. You can have a lot of fun writing about your own travel experiences and adventures.

LOVE IT!

A WRITE PAGE

HELP
DESIGN
An
SUV

Twinkle, the star, needs your help designing a really neat **4 x 4 sports utility vehicle.** Below are some of the things he'd like to have. Add to them, if you like. You can draw your own designs below. Maybe you'd a sport-ute for around town. Maybe another for bashing around the boonies. *Have fun!*

- ☐ Big wheels
- ☐ Radio antenna
- ☐ Roof rack
- ☐ Two-tone paint

- ☐ Rooftop spotlight
- ☐ Extra gas can
- ☐ Pennant pole
- ☐ Rear view mirror

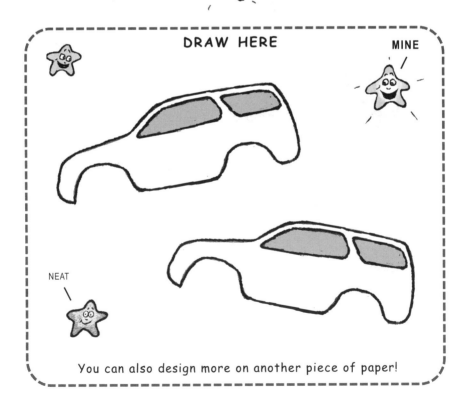

DRAW HERE   MINE

NEAT

You can also design more on another piece of paper!

MORE GAMES

AARGH!

WHAT FUN, CHARADES!

Am I going out of my mind? No, I'm only playing **charades!** Charades lets players act out all sorts of fun things **without** saying any words. The other players get to guess what the player is trying to tell them.

1. To start charades, the player chooses a **category**. This can be movie, TV or rock stars, favorite cartoon characters, titles of movie or TV programs, popular book titles, popular sayings or song titles.

2. The player holds up the number of **fingers** for the **words** of the category. A four-word movie, for example, would take four fingers.

3. The player then holds up **one finger**, indicating the **first word**. He or she then acts out the word.

HAIRY..THEN A POT...THEN A HER. GIVE ME A CLUE!*

4. If the name or title is one word, it can be broken into **syllables**. For example, let's say you have chosen one-word name to do a charade on. You'd say **name** and hold up **one finger**. To indicate the syllables, you'd hold up fingers to show the number. When the players get the syllable, you can nod and then hold up two fingers for the second syllable. *Fun, huh?*

*HARRY POTTER (BOOK)

WHAT ARE YOU DOING? *NOTHING!*

So you're just sitting around, with nothing to do. Here are **ten things** to do in a hotel or motel room when you're wondering what you could do that's fun, without making too much noise. Try not to get so excited that you yell. That sort of spoils the object of these games.

1/ GO FLY: Toss the **paper airplane** you made earlier across the room, trying to hit a target like a chair, a suitcase, or a plastic glass (see the *Flying Fun with Paper Airplanes* chapter). Haven't made a paper airplane yet? Now's a great time.

2. DROP ZONE: Put a plastic cup on the floor, between your feet. While standing, drop a penny from eye level, trying to get the penny in the glass.

3. DEPTH CHARGE: Put a plastic cup in an empty ice bucket. Fill the bucket with water above the top of the cup. Drop a penny and see if you can get it to drop into the glass.

4.FINGER FUN: Close your eyes and try to touch the tip of your **nose** with your **finger**. Not so easy, is it?

5. TONGUE TRY: Try to touch the tip of your **nose** with your **tongue**. Not so easy, is it?

6. BACKWARD COUNT: Count backwards. Start with a number you can easily reach counting forward, like 10, 25 or 100.

7. BACKWARD ALPHA-BET: Recite the **alphabet** backwards. Goodluck!

8. DRAWING BLINDFOLD-ED: Get some paper and a pencil. Have someone lightly **blindfold you** and then you try to **draw** a picture. You can draw something from memory that's in your room, such as a shoe, a watch, or a chair. Or you can draw something you know in your imagination, like a dog or a car or an elephant.

9. THE BLINDFOLDED POINTER: Have someone lightly **blindfold** you and then turn you around three times. See if you can correctly point to objects in the room, like the bed, the bathroom, the mirror, a chair, etc. You'd be surprised.

10. TOUCHY, FEELY: Have an adult **hide** a familiar and safe object in a **sock**. This can be a comb, a ring, a watch, a pen, or a ball.Or something like that. Then by **feeling** through the sock, try to guess what the object is. *Be brave.*

WHERE
IZIT?

The Izit Game: The first player takes a map and picks a **town, city or place** in the direction you're going. The player gives a clue, such as "this is a city between Sunnydale and Mayberry on the road we're on," and then challenges:

"Where Izit?"+

The other players then try to find the location that has been selected. Each town, city or place should be within about 50 miles of where you are and should be easy to find.

Upgraded Izzit: If you're heading for a town, for example, you can ask them to find a particular thing, such as a park or a river on a map. Or, if you're out on a freeway, you can ask them to find the next rest stop. This sometimes is particularly interesting if you have been on the road a while.

*Translation: *Where Is It?*

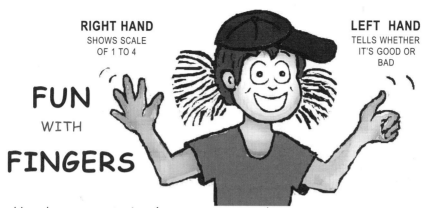

RIGHT HAND
SHOWS SCALE
OF 1 TO 4

LEFT HAND
TELLS WHETHER
IT'S GOOD OR
BAD

FUN
WITH
FINGERS

Here's a secret sign language you and your companions can share. You can tell each other how well you like or dislike things. All without words.

RIGHT HAND
With left hand **THUMB UP**

4 FINGERS: Can't get much better than this. Your best rating!
3 FINGERS: Way cool!
2 FINGERS: Okay, but sort of so-so
1 FINGER: A yawner. Good one to stay away from. Least favorable of good ratings.

LEFT HAND
Controls **winner** or looser **status**

Thumb UP
GOOD! A winner

Thumb DOWN
Not good.
A bummer.

RIGHT HAND
With left hand **THUMB DOWN**

4 FINGERS: Barfo. Bummer to the max. Your worst rating!
3 FINGERS: Grosses me out!
2 FINGERS: Pretty bad. May have some good qualities, but these elude me right now.
1 FINGER: Really not good. Bummer.

THAT'S A BIG THUMBS UP. WAY UP.

OH, NO!
NOT
THOSE
GAMES!

Horrors! Here are some special games that you can have fun with on a long trip

ONLY YES OR NO?

Here's a game that will drive you *wild*. That's because, no matter what anyone asks or says in a conversation in the next your, no one can say **yes** or **no**. You can answer, of course. But you can't say **yes or no**. Got the idea? The fun comes when people forget not to use the no-no words (yes or no) or get tricked into using them. But you wouldn't do that, *would you?*
Hint: you can vary the game by putting your own time limit on how long to play. Or what penalties those who forget the game will have, if they miss.

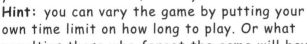

FUNNY YOU SHOULD ASK THAT

You set up a certain **answer** that players have to answer questions with. *No matter what.* The results can be amazing.

For example, if you pick the phrase, *"who cut the cheese?"* to be the answer to everything, then all your players have to answer anything they're asked *with that phrase*. For example, if someone asks, "Do you want to stop for ice cream?" the player **can't answer** yes or no but only, *"who cut the cheese?"* Get the idea?

Hint: It's loads of fun when you assign different **phrases** to different players. Make up your phrases in advance.

SPECIAL
MEMORIES

Draw a picture of
someone or something
you'd really like to
remember from this trip

A DRAW PAGE

A FEW WORDS ABOUT WHAT I DREW

_____

_____

HURRY UP
SUNDOWN

When will the **sun go down?** On vacation, the days are long and beautiful, but sunset can be a special time. To play this game, everyone picks a **time** when when the sun is fully down and out of view. Someone with a watch determines the winner.

WRITE DOWN
YOUR GUESSES

1.———————   2.———————
3.———————   4.———————

Each player picks a number and after each number writes in their guess on THE EXACT TIME when the sun will be fully set.

Note: the game is over when the sun is **fully out of view.** Be certain not to look directly into the setting sun to prevent any possible eye damage.

Other variations: You can take turns naming the many **colors** of the sky as the sun goes down. Red, gold, blue purple. You might see these and many more beautiful colors. *Just look for them.*

MY SPECIAL SUNSET MEMORY

Sunsets are special. Draw a picture of a favorite sundown you enjoyed during your trip.

HURRY! I'M FADING FAST

A DRAW PAGE

I'LL BE BACK

ABOUT MY SUNSET

WHAT'S DIFFERENT?

Have fun testing your powers of observation

Look closely at the two pictures on these two pages. See if you can see ten differences in the two pictures. Got them? Okay, now: On the right picture, locator letters (top row) and numbers (on the left) will tell you where to look. Then you can see the answers. Did you get all ten?

You're traveling down the road and you blink. Something's different between your first look (left) and your second (below). What happened? See if you can find 10 differences.

ANSWERS: *Whoa!* The **birds** (1B)have gotten more numerous. Now there are 6 of them. And where's the sun? Now there are **clouds** and it's **raining** (E-J; 1-3). And what happened to that **silo** beside the farmhouse? And did you notice that **castle** before (F4)? And that herd of cows has increased. Wait a minute: how'd that **dinosaur** get in there? (J5). And that field of flowers has been replaced by a **lake** (7 H-J). What's that cow doing in the rear view **mirror** (C4)? And the mouse looking out the window(A5). Boy, a lot can happen in just the blink of the eye when you're traveling. So you better stay alert.

I HAVE SOME

MY FINAL WORDS
ON THIS
TRIP

Did you have a good time? What did you especially like?
Or what didn't you like? Sum up a few words to help you
remember this trip. And below, be sure to rate it.

AGAIN, NEXT
YEAR?
Please?

On a scale of 1 (worst) to 10 (best),
I'd rate this trip a big fat: _____